A.F. Harrold is an English poet w|
for both adults and children. He h
visiting schools, running workshops
poem-stuff with and for kids at un
the morning. He is the owner of ma _..., a handful
of hats, a few good ideas and one beard. Besides
various books of poetry for adults he has also written a
number children's novels including the **Fizzlebert Stump**
series (illustrated by Sarah Horne) and **The Imaginary**
(illustrated by Emily Gravett), which are published by
Bloomsbury.

Chris Riddell is the creator of an extraordinary range of
books which have won many illustration awards including
the UNESCO Prize, the Greenaway Medal (twice) and
the Hay Festival Medal for Illustration. His work includes
the highly-acclaimed Ottoline titles and the 2013 Costa
Children's Book Award-winning **Goth Girl and the Ghost
of a Mouse**. Chris is also a renowned political cartoonist
whose work appears in the Observer, the Literary Review
and the New Statesman. He was appointed Children's
Laureate in 2015.

VIVI H

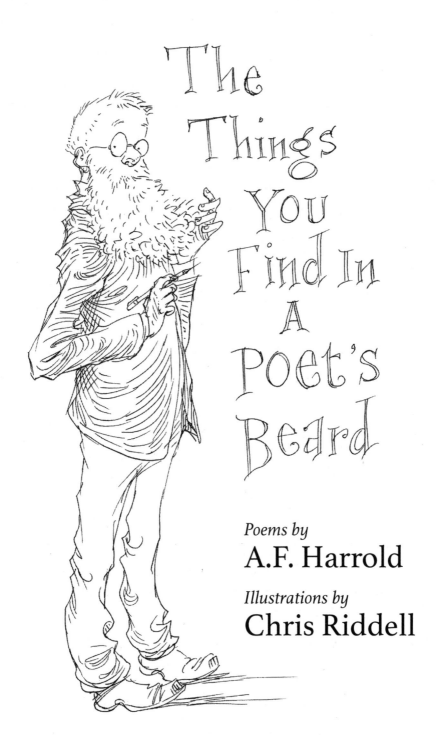

The Things You Find In A Poet's Beard

Poems by
A.F. Harrold

Illustrations by
Chris Riddell

Burning Eye

Acknowledgements: Some of these poems have been previously published: *Postcards From the Hedgehog* in **Postcards From The Hedgehog** (Two Rivers Press, 2007); *Jam* and *A Christmas Poem* in **The Man Who Spent Years In The Bath** (Quirkstandard's Alternative, 2008); *Jam, The Iced-Bun Song, A Poem About A Dog Having A Bath, A Menagerie of Animals, A Nice Tune, Jennifer Jones, Poetry and the Dragon, Pirates, Yo Ho Ho and a Bottle of Diet Coke Please…, Not The Best Poem in The World, If I Woke Up As A Beetle, A Poem About Some Food, Midnight Feasting, I Want To Be a Wallaby* and *The Visitation* in **I Eat Squirrels** (Quirkstandard's Alternative, 2009); *Birdlife, Dreams, Spring Poem* and *A Story Poem* in **Lies My Mother Never Told Me** (Burning Eye Books, 2014).

Typeset by Dominic Brookman
using Dyslexie (dyslexiefont.com)

This edition published by Burning Eye Books 2015
www.burningeye.co.uk

@burningeyebooks

Burning Eye Books
15 West Hill, Portishead, BS20 6LG

ISBN 978 1 90913 6 618

Dedicated to
James Carter, Bernard O'Donoghue and John Hegley,
lovely beardless poets the lot of 'em.

Contents

The Things You Find In A Poet's Beard 10
Jam 12
Jammie Dodgers Aren't The Only Fruit 13
The New Farmer Learns 14
Bangers 14
Burger Tips 15
Piece of Pie 15
The Iced-Bun Song 16
The Ambitious Spider 17
The Asthmatic Racer 18
The Tennis Player's Complaint 18
The Fastest Man In The World
Does The Washing Up 19
Nine Events For An Alternative Olympics 19
Three Pets 20
Kitten-Man, Crime-Fighter 21
A Poem About a Dog Having a Bath 22
Dog Food 23
Burying The Dog In The Garden 24
Birdlife 25
Smaller Ones Are Better 26
A Menagerie Of Animals 28
Trees Are (Somewhat) Rubbish 30
In The Tree's Defence 31
Can't See The Tree 32
Questions, Questions 33
Here, There, Everywhere 34
The Flavour Of Night 35
Dreams 36
Dreamless 37
The Perils of Breakfast 38
Two Quick Tips 40
School 41
Snow Today, Gone Tomorrow 41
Socks Poem 42
Tiger Socks 43
Penelope's Hats 44
A Nice Tune 45
Jennifer Jones 46
Stephen Slowcoach 47
My Best Mate 48

Contents

The Picking Of Graham Pendlebury's Nose 50
Samantha's Rainy Day Activities 52
Teeth 53
Lesser Known, But Not Less Important 54
Bears and Bees (A Song) 56
Business As Usual 57
Grandma 59
The Warning 60
February 61
Two Spring Poems 62
Poetry & The Dragon 63
A Christmas Poem 66
A Poem For My Mum 68
In The Dark 69
The Taste Of A Biscuit 70
Flowers 72
Alphapoem 73
Troll Song 74
Raindrops Keep Falling Out Of Bed 76
Pirates 78
Yo Ho Ho and a Bottle of Diet Coke
Please If You Don't Mind, Thank You
Ever So Much (a poem for polite pirates) 78
Some Mistakes 80
Not The Best Poem In The World 80
Some Simple Solutions For The Nervous 81
Not Exactly A Love Letter 82
A Story Poem 83
Horrible Poem 84
Some Wigyiig Facts 86
If I Woke Up As A Beetle 87
My Mad Uncle, My Aunts and The Endless Scarf 88
Postcards From The Hedgehog 90
Psychic 92
A Poem About Some Food 94
Midnight Feasting 96
Song Of The Fussy Eater 98
I Want To Be A Wallaby (Or A Kangaroo) 100
The Visitation 102
Outside 103

The Things You Find In A Poet's Beard

The Things You Find
In A Poet's Beard

There are fleas and flies and knots and nits,
breadcrumbs, marmite stains and bits

of pencils lost in the distant past,
coffee dribbles from a thermos flask.

Spiders' webs and sparrows' nests,
string that they use for old men's vests,

bits of dinner from yesterday,
orange pips and strips of hay.

Chips glued in with tomato ketchup.
Bits of driftwood sometimes fetch up

and tangle about in the twisty hair
the poet grows on his chin and there

are knitting needles, lengths of twine...
Oh no! Hang on! That's a porcupine.

Koala bears peer out and chew,
there's a cockatiel and a cockatoo.

A sloth blinks slowly under the fur
and if you listen close there's a happy purr.

•

It happened once that Sir Simon Bungle
became entangled in the furry jungle.

He tripped while walking by the poet,
tripped and slipped and who would know it,

he fell head first into the beard.
Inside was just as he had feared —

dark like a forest and ticklish too
so he simply did what he had to do...

He was trained by the army, had been to the pole,
was an expert in survival and that rigmarole.

So, he ate all the chips (of which there were nine),
wove himself a ladder out of string and twine

and after exploring around and about
he let down the ladder and he climbed straight out.

.

So, it's thanks to Sir Simon that we've seen inside
the beard of a poet and there's nothing left to hide.

It's dark and dangerous and terribly weird,
and even by the bravest is sensibly feared.

So be well-warned (as a child well-reared):
never get entangled in a poet's beard.

Jam

What are Jammie Dodgers dodging?

Presumably stuff that would otherwise lodge in
the jam in the middle
or the biscuity bit.

I guess that's it.

Jammie Dodgers Aren't The Only Fruit

Biscuits come in many shapes.

Some are shaped like the sun.
Some are shaped like a Frisbee.
Some are shaped like a plate.
Some are shaped like a coin.
Some are shaped like a discus.
Some are shaped like a flying saucer.
Some are shaped like a non-flying saucer.
Some are shaped like a full moon.
Some are shaped like a clock face.
Some are shaped like the face of a sundial.
Some are shaped like the face of a person with a face
                              shaped like a Jammie Dodger.

And that's just the round ones.

The New Farmer Learns

I wish I'd then known then
   what I now know now —
that it's eggs from the chickens
   and milk from the cow.

You see, my first day was rainy,
   but worse than that —
I drank chicken juice
   with a soft-boiled pat.

Bangers

I watch the sausages
running
carefree in the field.

It's a sad thought to think
soon
they'll be in my sandwich.

Burger Tips

Brown and crispy dripping with juice:
I like my burgers made from moose,

but little bones can make you cough
so I always saw the antlers off.

Piece of Pie

A chap called Simon
met a pie-man
going to the fair.

He bought a pie
for a reasonable price
and ate it. Right there.

Nothing funny happened.
Nothing weird occurred.

Or at least
that's the story I heard.

The Iced-Bun Song

Five iced-buns in the baker's shop.
One of them is sold to feed a hungry cop.

Four iced-buns on the baker's shelf.
One of them goes to a party with an elf.

Three iced-buns getting lonelier each day.
One gets a part in a Shakespeare play.

Two iced-buns in the baker's window.
One gets promoted: becomes a flamingo.

One iced-bun left all on its own
talks to the other iced-buns on the phone.

The Ambitious Spider

There's a spider in the bath
and it isn't catching flies.
It's more ambitious than that,
you can see it in all eight eyes.

It spins the stickiest webs
in the gap between the taps,
and all around the overflow,
with the hope that maybe, perhaps

while you are having your bath
you'll waggle your feet in the air,
and get tangled up in the webbing
and get stuck in the spider's snare.

Unable to escape
it'll wander up to your nose
and begin to nibble from there,
right down to your entrapped toes.

All they will find in the morning
is a bathtub filled with bones,
and a spider the size of a swan
emitting satisfied groans.

But it's easy, of course, to be safe,
to avoid the spider's traps:
just share your bath with a buddy,
and make them take the end with the taps.

The Asthmatic Racer

When I run I wheeze.

I run a bit more
then I lean on my knees
and wheeze.

When I tell them I'm just resting
they say that they're drug testing
and they take away the
canister from my inhaler

which leaves me
increasingly wheezy
which doesn't please me.

And if I run after that
I tend to fall flat.

The Tennis Player's Complaint

'You'd think we still lived in the dark ages.
I mean, yes, I'm a lady, but heavens above!

My racket will cause him an injury soon
if that umpire keeps calling me "Love".'

The Fastest Man In The World Does The Washing Up

'I've finished.'

'What really? When?'

'While you were writing the title.'

'Oh, goodness. You are fast, aren't you?'

'Yes.'

'Well, thank you, that's very kind. I'll put the kettle on. Would you like a cup of tea?'

'Just a quick one, thank you.'

Nine Events For An Alternative Olympics

Discus discussing.

Tug-of-war skipping.

Synchronised javelin juggling.

Kangaroo cuddling.

The combined long jump and building a sandcastle.

The 200 metres custard swim.

The 400 metres knit.

The 100 metres stroll.

Competitive tickling.

Three Pets

i.
A pet cheetah won't ever be beaten.
If you dare win a race, prepare to be eaten.

ii.
There's nothing quite as scary
as an overweight canary.

If it weighs more than you do,
you'll be knee deep in doo-doo.

iii.
You can't teach
a leech
to jump through hoops
or turn somersaults
or chase a stick.

In fact,
as a pet
it might seem a disappointment,
but it does have one advantage:

it won't need expensive pet food.
To the leech your arm looks pretty good,
filled as it is with warm thick blood.

Kitten-Man, Crime-Fighter

'I have been bitten
by a radioactive kitten.

My superpower
is to distract villains
by being so cute
they have to stop robbing the bank
in order to tickle me under the chin

and when they do
I do them in.

With one swipe of my tiny paws
(with their even tinier, but still sharp, claws)
I snag their trouser leg.

And if the criminal lingers
I bite my tiny teeth down on their fingers
and nip them quite hard.

Then, once they've given in
the police come and make the arrest.

They throw the book at them,
the key away
and some dried food in a bowl for me.

I relax in the evening
playing manically
with a man-size ball of wool
until my mum puts me out for the night.'

A Poem About a Dog Having a Bath

The dog in the bathroom is starting to bark.
He spent the afternoon playing games in the park,
chasing every stick and every thrown ball
and rolling in the puddles, both the big and the small.

When it started raining and the mud splashed up
he started rolling around like an excitable pup
who'd never seen a muddy, mucky bit of ground before.
He got dirty as a dog can get, and then he got more.

But now he's come home, we're indoors in the dry,
and up in the bathroom he begins to cry
as Mum attempts to clean the caked mud
and the twigs and the grit and she goes scrub, scrub,
                                            scrub.

But he makes an awful fuss and he makes an awful row,
and it's woof, bark, bark, yelp, grrr, yelp, growl,
and it's bark, yelp, woof, grunt, growl, bark, howl,
'cause she's got soap in his eyes and he can't reach
                                            the towel

because he's a dog and his arms are not long
and with paws instead of hands he couldn't hold on
to the towel anyway, so he barks and he cries
(as any dog would do who got soap in their eyes).

But he'll get his own back on Mum in a minute.
When it's time to dry him off, she tries to begin it
by rubbing him dry, but he makes a quick break
and runs into her bedroom for a good old shake.

Dog Food

Aged six and a half
Algernon wanted a dog
desperately.

One day he came home from school
and his mum said,
'Go look in the garden, Algie.'

In the middle of the lawn
was a tin of dog food.

The label was torn in such a way
that the word 'food' was missing.
It just said, 'Dog'.

Although Algernon
wasn't fooled into thinking
this was actually a pet dog

he went inside and thanked his mum.
After all,
she had gone to some effort.

He pretended to be happy with his new pet.
He tied a lead round the can's neck
and took it for a walk.

In his back pocket
was the can opener
he'd borrowed from the kitchen drawer.

When he got to the park
he slid the opener's blade round the can's top
and let all the meaty goodness out.

Pretty soon he was surrounded
('surhounded' you might say)
by springy tail-wagging dogs of various kinds.

They were all very friendly
and their owners
let Algernon throw sticks for them.

It was the best afternoon in the park
he'd spent since he'd watched
bread being thrown at the ducks.

Although he still had no pet of his own
to take home,
he didn't grumble, after all

his mum promised to buy him a new can
every weekend,
which was almost as good.

Burying The Dog In The Garden

We buried the dog in the garden,
  where it had buried its bones,
we patted the earth down neatly
  and piled up some stones.

When mum saw what we'd done
  she made us dig him up quick,
he was only asleep when we buried him
  but now he's looking quite sick.

Birdlife

Impressed
by their singing,
their feathers
and their flying,
Simon climbed
his garden's tree
and built a nest
in the branches.

He gobbled worms
and sang joyously
at the sun's rising.

He flew, arms out,
with enthusiastic
amounts of flapping.

Nevertheless
featherless
he fell
and
(caught by the cat)
that was that.

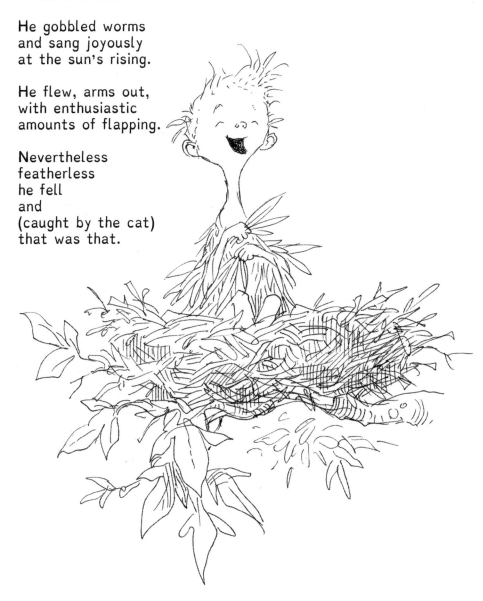

Smaller Ones Are Better

Never get a pet bigger than yourself —
oversized animals are bad for your health —

take a snake that could swallow you whole —
a great white shark won't fit a fish-bowl —

you might try to keep a polar bear in the freezer,
but don't tell your mum, 'cause the news wouldn't
                                        please her —

a bottlenose dolphin hogs the bath —
a big butch hyena is good for a laugh

but when it gets peckish, starts looking for lunch,
the last sound you'll hear is a mighty meaty munch —

and it's the same with a tiger, the same with a lion —
don't get a walrus, and don't think of trying

to befriend a blue whale — they're bigger than buses —
and when the food bill arrives, then you'll see what a
                                        fuss is —

don't get a pet bigger than a person —
smaller ones are better — you bet you'd start cursing

if you had to clear up all the mess that you find
fallen to the floor from an elephant's behind —

a rhinoceros might be a tough old trooper
but it tends to overwork the tired pooper-scooper —

stick to a stick-insect, stick with the cat,
befriend a little rabbit or a mouse or a rat

or a sensible dog or a gerbil or a parrot
or smallest and safest — a crunchy tender carrot.

A Menagerie Of Animals

i.
Great grey belly porker,
toothy yawning slug,
cow-nosed submarine,
giant in the mud,
unlikely ballerina
tip-toes underwater,
sleepy swampland-island,
river's favourite daughter.

ii.
Stripy-armoured tiny tiger,
pollen-pouched and humble,
a fairy-small furry flyer,
content to simply bumble.

iii.
An African agitator,
sleeping now, snapping later.
Living log with beady eyes,
a flash of jaws and something dies.

Antelope and sleek gazelle
know the dangers very well,
are careful by the river Nile's
toothy and serrated smiles.

iv.
Fish-chasing waiters,
waddling torpedoes,
ice-footed flipper-flappers,
swimmers with no speedos.

v.
Knitting hunter,
insect hater —
catch them now,
eat them later.

vi.
Orange as a sunset,
red as a pillar-box.
Entering the chicken coop,
unwelcome as Goldilocks.

vii.
As big as houses end to end,
glimpsed and then it's gone,
an island for the mariner
he won't step foot upon.

A water feature fountaining
between the foaming waves,
an oily mountain sinking fast,
takes plankton to their graves.

viii.
Purr-bearer,
fur-wearer,
tail-tosser,
mouse-bosser.

ix.
At first a dot,
then a hop.

Trees Are (Somewhat) Rubbish

They always say, 'Money doesn't grow on trees,'
and they're right.
But that's not the whole story, is it?

Why don't they ever mention the other things?
Like bicycles, lampshades and bears?
Trees are rubbish at growing these, too.

Not to mention statues of angels,
songs about coughing so much you fall asleep,
or frogs, badgers or sheep.

And then there's crockery, sausages, televisions,
shoes and apricots.
These don't grow on trees either.

(Except for apricots.)

In The Tree's Defence

Trees are good at what they do,
at being oak or beech or yew.

They shake their leaves to make a breeze
and pop out blossom for the bees.

In crook of branch they'll hold a nest
which, birds concur, is for the best.

On rainy days they shield the feller
who's forgot his umbrella.

In summer they provide the shade
for picnickers out in the glade.

Inside their sturdy hearts of wood
trees are simply doing good.

Can't See The Tree...

Charles made a tree
out of bits of wood.

It looked pretty good.
It had leaves.
It had squirrels.
It was in a forest.

It was so good, in fact,
when he turned away
and turned back
he couldn't tell
which tree was his.

Which was quite annoying
since he'd put
so much effort into making it.

Questions, Questions

How d'you fit a genie in a bottle?
How d'you fit a world inside a book?
How d'you fit the sun into the summer?
How d'you fit a mountain in one look?

How d'you fit an oak inside an acorn?
How d'you fit the wind under a kite?
How d'you fit your sweetheart in a locket?
How d'you fit the dark into the night?

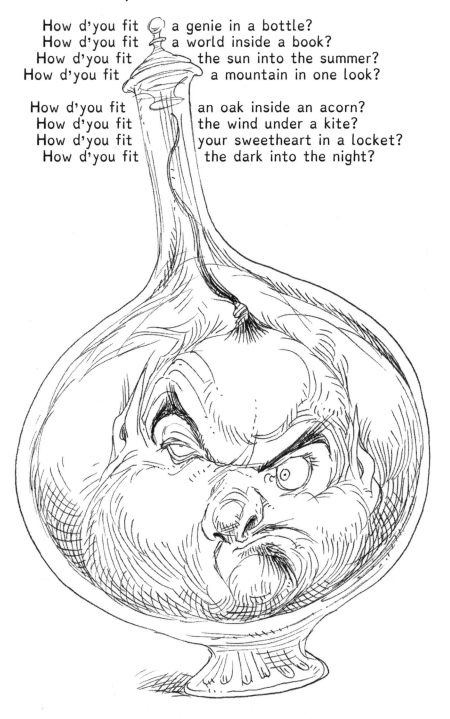

Here, There, Everywhere

On the one hand,
buses know they're better
than trains.
Buses replace trains,
never the other way around.

On the other hand,
trains look down on buses,
waiting for engine trouble
and a level crossing
to teach them who's boss.

On the third hand,
planes look down on everyone.

The Flavour Of Night

It tastes of high clouds
   of crisp cold
      of twilight

It tastes of autumn leaves
   of bonfires
      of the first star

It tastes of curtains
   of 'Time for bed'
      of warm pillows

It tastes of snuggled up
   of stories
      of snoring

It tastes of unbelievable
   of muddled up
      of brilliance

It tastes of marzipan
   of early glow
      of morning duvet

It tastes of half-awake
   of alarm clock
      of breakfast

Dreams

They sleep during the hottest part of the day,
when it's brightest
and when the curtains are at their thinnest.

They don't sleep well.
The room is stuffy. The windows are shut.
Everybody else is out at work.

They wriggle about, push the sheets away,
turn the pillow over and over
trying to find the other side.

It's no wonder, then, when night falls
and they button up their overcoats
and lace up their soft shoes

and, packed supper in hand,
climb inside our heads
to go to work,

that they make little sense.
After an anxious stifled sleepless day,
in the cool muddle of the night,

the dreams begin to yawn.
Their eyelids droop and their heads loll.
In the middle of telling one story

they sit up suddenly,
saying, 'I wasn't asleep!'
and start off down a completely different path.

Dreamless

It's a long night
that has no dreams in it.

It's a long dark night
without the movie show
rolling round your head.

It's a long dark dull night
without unexpected
unexplained
unlikely adventures,

such as flying over the town
startling starlings
and perplexing pigeons,

or eating all the cakes
the baker bakes
and scoffing all the sweets
and chocolate treats
that litter the dreamer's streets.

It's a dull night
with no dreams in.

Just darkness from dusk
to morning's first light,
and the sound of snoring
and the smell of duvet.

It's a dull day
with no dreams in either.

The Perils of Breakfast

Watch out for bears in your cornflakes.

They're dangerous.
They have big claws.
They are always hungry.
At breakfast time, doubly so.

If you lift a spoonful of cornflakes to your mouth
and it's got a bear hiding in it,
well,
you'll be in trouble. Won't you?
Eaten up just like that.
Gobble. Gobble. Crunch.

Fortunately
bears are larger than cornflakes
and so you can usually spot
a bit of fur poking round the side.

If you do,
put your spoon down
and choose something else instead.

But,
watch out for crocodiles in your porridge.
Watch out for tigers under your toast.

Two Quick Tips

Never go shoplifting.
They're heavy things
and one accidental slip
might lead to a drop of the shop
and could chop
off a fingertip or two.

On the other hand,
never go shiplofting either.
Hoisting a boat in the air
will drop seaweed in your hair,
barnacles on your head
and if your scarf gets caught
in the propellers, kid, you're dead.

School

In my day school was very different.

For one thing,
there wasn't so much history to learn.
Lots of things that have happened now
hadn't happened back then.

For another thing,
the teachers were much younger.
Look at your teacher and take twenty
or thirty years off...
why, they were probably kids themselves.

Snow Today, Gone Tomorrow

Snow thaws and eaves drip,
snowman lilts and sags and dips,
his carrot nose
is nicked by crows,
his scarf's reclaimed by mum.

Footprints fade with melting snow,
to slush that special landscape goes,
sleds are shedded,
school is dreaded,
grownups happy, kids grow glum.

Socks Poem

Don't mock
the humble sock.

Even a sock that's old
will keep your feet from feeling cold.

Though if it's got a hole
in the toe or the heel or the sole

it might be more breezy,
mending it is easy:

put on your special sewing smock
and darn that sock.

A sock with eyes
is a sock in disguise.

Put on the hand it might be a snake
a giraffe or worm or ape,

or other creation
of the sock-puppet master's imagination.

Me? I prefer to keep
my socks on my feet.

The ones I like are the types
with stripes.

Tiger Socks

When Philip wears his orange stripy socks,
his lucky socks,
his these-make-me-feel-strong-and-plucky socks,
he roars on the inside.

He feels ten feet tall
and dangerous and brave and confident and able to do
just about anything.

Philip feels like he has the heart of a tiger
singing up from his tiger-striped feet
and as he walks
he feels the low slink of the tiger in his shoulders,
the slow blink of the tiger in his eyes.

No one messes with him when he's in his lucky socks.
He can do anything,
  achieve anything,
    stand up to anyone.

No bully can beat him,
no lesson defeat him,

except history,
historically that's never been a tiger's strong point.

Or maths.

Penelope's Hats

Aunt Penelope really doesn't like hats,
  she wears cushions up there instead.
She says they are warm in the winter
  and soft if she falls on her head.

But cushions and pillows are no good
  to wear on your head in the rain.
Like sponges they fill up with water
  and for hours they drip as they drain.

So Penelope wears, when it's raining,
  a duck (one leg tied to each ear).
It's waterproof, and uncomplaining,
  she says, except when given to fear.

In thunderstorms, when all the lightning
  flashes and crashes all night,
the poor duck will quack in a frenzy
  and flap wings with all of its might.

And sometimes, if Penny is running,
  the flapping's enough to take flight,
and the duck and the aunt will go soaring
  up into the sky out of sight.

A Nice Tune

When Sidney the snake
decided to take
piano lessons
they lasted seconds.

Headbutting the keys
didn't please
Mrs Hosannah
who owned the piano.

She slammed the lid
which did for Sid.

Jennifer Jones

Jennifer Jones was a wonderful girl,
  her cheeks were rosy, her hair would curl,
she'd skip about and sing and laugh
  but on Friday nights she had her bath.

When her mother said, 'Jenny, I'm running the water,'
  a change came over her beautiful daughter.
She'd throw back her head and let out a shout
  that would aggravate her granddad's gout.

Her hair would spike, she'd go red in the face,
  she'd jump and she'd jump all over the place,
knocking down vases and scaring the cat,
  the goldfish, the duck and her brother's pet rat.

Her mother gave up and just got in herself
  and had a long soak, which is good for the health.

.

Jennifer Jones is now nearly thirty
  and has no friends at all because she's so dirty.

Stephen Slowcoach

It wasn't that Stephen was slow.
He was slower than that.
In fact, he was late.

By the time he finished his dinner
the washing up had already been done.

By the time he got dressed
it was time for bed.

By the time he got to sleep
it was time for breakfast.

By the time he tied his shoelaces
he'd outgrown his shoes.

By the time he talked his mum into getting a kitten
it was a cat.

By the time he finished sharpening his pencil
a tree had grown from the other end.

By the time he put his hand up to answer a question
the other kids had gone home.

By the time he finished the egg and spoon race
he was walking hand in wing with a chicken.

By the time he kissed his mum goodbye
she was back again.

By the time he crossed the road
the green man had turned red.

So now, Stephen's dead.

My Best Mate

He's eight feet tall.
He's got blue hair.
He's got gaps in his teeth
and a dead scary stare.

He's got wild ideas.
He's got magic powers.
He's got jokes that go on
for hours and hours.

He's ever so tough.
He's ever so clever.
He's thunder and lightning,
he's dangerous weather.

He knows about storms.
He's flown in them too.
He wrestled a lion
when we went to the zoo.

He waits outside school
and he walks me home.
With my best mate there
I'm don't feel alone.

You say you can't see him?
Don't believe he's there?
Well me and my mate,
see, we really don't care.

The Picking Of Graham Pendlebury's Nose

'What goes up, must come down,'

said the doctor,
to Graham's mother
who was looking worried.

Graham
was also worried.
He'd pushed a bit too hard
on that last pick
and now
could feel his brain
pressed up against his fingertip.
He was afraid
if he pulled his finger out
his brain
would drain.

The doctor gave Graham's arm another tug
but the boy's delving digit wouldn't budge.
It was well wedged
in his head.

'If it went all the way in,' the doctor said,
'it should come all the way out again.'

'My brain!' Graham shouted, 'my brain!'

'Don't be so silly,' the doctor snapped.

Later, x-rays proved
that the doctor was wrong
and Graham was right
and ever since that night
he's lived with a finger up one nostril.

Of course, his life is very different now
to how it was before
'The Nose Incident.'

He's had to learn to write left-handed, for instance,
and to eat with one piece of cutlery at a time,
and spring and flowers and bread and girls
don't smell as nice as once they did,
but he gets on okay.

Once a week he leans backwards
and pulls his finger out
to give the nail a trim
and then, quickly, puts it back in.

Samantha's Rainy Day Activities

Samantha
very carefully
laid out her paints,

put on
her father's best shirt,
back to front,

chose one paintbrush
out of the many
in the jar,

adjusted
the angle of her beret,
squinted,

and began
to paint
the cat.

Now,
on the fridge door is a photo
of a purple cat,

and a bill
from the dry cleaners
for a difficult job well done.

Teeth

Shirley was six when her teeth started to fall out.
Her big brother, Ben, told her not to worry.
He said it had happened to him,
he said it happened to everyone,
and told her she'd get new teeth in time.

In fact, to prove his point
and to set her mind at ease
he snuck her into their gran's bedroom one night
and by the light of a small torch
showed her the dentures floating in the bedside glass.

Ben told Shirley that soon enough
their mum would take her to the dentist's
to be fitted with dentures of her own —
a clanky toothy plastic plate
Shirley was sure she would hate to have to wear.

She cried and cried when a second tooth became wobbly
and her mum asked her what the matter was
and Shirley explained between fearful sobs
and her mum said that Ben, even though he was her son,
was just an idiot.

Of course, new teeth grew from underneath
where her milk teeth had been
and she told her brother Ben that she wouldn't need
                                    false teeth,
not for years and years, although if he played a trick
                                    like that again
he might be needing them that much sooner.

Lesser Known, But Not Less Important

If you think the Tooth Fairy has it tough
spare a thought for the Finger Nail Pixie
who has to collect cast off nail clippings.

And then there's the Ear Wax Leprechaun
who scrapes the topsides of pillows
and the Left Over Elf who scrapes plates.

Not forgetting the poor old Bogey Boggart
and the dread-inducing Dandruff Banshee
whose screams foretell a fall of hair snow.

Looking sad's the Belly-Button Fluff Gargoyle
who waits on rooftops to collect drifting fluff,
of which, up there, there's never very much.

And finally there's the pesky Eyeball Sprite
who collects eyeballs that fall out in the night.
He catches them in his silky paws and juggles.

Bears and Bees (A Song)

There are two bears in the beehive
  and the bees will not behave.
The bears are that much bigger
  and the bees are barely brave.

The pair of big fat brown bears
  boldly bash the hive to bits.
The bees just buzz about them
  like bumbling stripy twits.

Buzz. Buzz. Buzz. Buzz.
(They're guzzling honeycomb.)
Buzz. Buzz. Buzz. Buzz.
(They're guzzling honeycomb.)

The bears have bulging bellies
  and they've honey in their fur.
(The bears have bulging bellies now,
  and honey in their fur.)

Never use honeycomb as a comb.
Never use honeycomb as a comb.
Never use honeycomb as a comb.
Never use honeycomb as a comb.

It sticks.

It tugs.

It leaves you with sweet smelling bald patches.

Business As Usual

The sun is shining very bright tonight.
The dog has laid its eggs up in the tree.
Wasps are sending birthday cards to you.
Everything is as it's meant to be.

The pelicans are travelling by taxi.
The penguins are dressing quite informal.
Lions are eating a meal of veggie mince.
Everything is absolutely normal.

The flowers are flying to the beehive.
The elephant is looking very small.
The cat is running itself a bubble bath.
There's nothing unusual here at all.

Grandma

If you say to your grandma
  Grandma, what big eyes you have
and she says
  All the better to see you with

And if you say to your grandma
  Grandma, what big ears you have
and she says
  All the better to hear you with

And you say
  Grandma, what a big nose you have
and she says
  All the better to smell you with

Don't ask about her teeth

Say instead
  Grandma, what lovely hair you have
Say
  Grandma, what a warm nightdress you have
Say
  Grandma, what neat knitting you have
Say
  Grandma, what a small but cosy cottage you have

Say anything, but don't mention her teeth

And all the time back away very slowly

And when you can,

hide

and use her mobile
(which is always on the table in the hall)
to text for help, very quietly

(remember the big ears)

The Warning

'Icy.'

'You see?'

'No, I said, 'Icy.''

'What do you see?'

'No. Icy, see?'

'You see the sea?'

'No. I see icy ice, see?'

'Uh?'

Push.
  Slip.
    Thump.
    Thunk.
                    S l i d   e.

'Icy, see?'

                              'Oh, yes. I see.'

February

Frost spins white lines
on the lawn,
grass turns glass-like,
crisp crackle-snap
underfoot.

Robins puff themselves,
look as big as tennis balls,
as light as dandelions,
tap on the bird bath's
ice rink concrete.

There's the doorbell.
A blue-lipped lady
wants to come in.
The doormat
flutters with snow.

Two Spring Poems

i.
After winter's chills
the daffodil's
spills
of sunbright
yellow light
brush the dust
out of the world's eyes.

ii.
Watch it fly
excitedly out of your hands,
explosively,
as a sudden bulb goes off,
a yellow trumpet blaring
so loud
so bright
it almost takes your eye out.

Poetry & The Dragon

If you open up my skull
   you won't see a brain in there,
underneath the skin and bone
   and bushy spreading hair
is something rather different,
   something quite unique,
something I must feed with fancy
   several times a week.

There's a dragon in my brain-box,
   puffing fire in my head,
it's always hungry, always thirsty,
   always must be fed
on images imagined,
   on truthful things and lies —
this dragon needs some stoking
   to puff its fire in my eyes.

I feed it with the glitter
   of dew on a spider's web,
no sooner is it noticed
   than it's gulped into my head —
I see the leaves of autumn
   turn yellow and red and fall —
the dragon takes everything I see,
   the dragon eats it all.

He swallows the shouting of people,
   angry in the street,
the roar of a jet down the valley
   is gobbled up like meat.
The smell of new bread baking,
   the green of the garden in spring,
the touch of a ghost at the back of my neck —
   the dragon eats everything.

He's kept alive by the world —
   by the sounds and the sights and the dreams,
he's got no ideas of his own, you see,
   but he's bulging at the seams —
he's fat with the pictures he's swallowed,
   huge on the noises he's heard —
from cheers in the playground football match
   to the squawk of grannie's bird —

that day when Mum was mad with me,
   and the day that I fell in love,
and other days that passed so slow,
   the hurt of the bully's shove,
the dream that I set foot on Mars,
   the clatter of Beowulf's fight —
all roll around in the dragon's maw,
   sparking and letting out light,

and once in a while he puffs up a flame,
   bursting with all he's eaten
and the images rush, they flutter and roar
   like runners who won't be beaten
in the race of memory, the race of words,
   of poetry flaming anew —
and I write it all down, one way or another,
   'cause that's what poets do.

A Christmas Poem

When my Great Aunt Bertha,
who was a Quaker,
read in the papers
of how their boys and our boys gave it all up,
put the guns down,
climbed over the top
and kicked the patched leather ball
between barbed wire and crater rims,
between the two straight dark ditches they lived in,
she took it upon herself to head down to Woolworth's
and buy up
all the marked down
boxes of Christmas cards
lolling on the January shelves.

She spent her war years licking stamps,
inking addresses,
printing xmas messages
in one of a number of different languages,
as appropriate,
signing her love
and visiting the pillar-box at the head of her road.
Sacks of the things went off at once,
whole stretches of trench filled with holly,
spade-handled robins,
magi, stockings and snow.
The babe of peace arrived in his manger,
in the stable,
in March, in April, in May,
ceaselessly,
year on year.

If there had been no calendars,
no officers, no orders,
no today's or yesterday's newspaper in the mess,
in the trench,
no date on the soldier's letter from home,
then her plan may have worked,
assuming the other side were equally ill-equipped
and open-mindedly eager to clutch peace as it passed.

But
no one was stupid enough
to think it might be Christmas
every day,
no one was fooled by her hand,
and besides,
the ball needed pumping
and a puncture repair kit.
Great Aunt Bertha.

A Poem For My Mum

I miss you
like the puddle misses the snowman it was
I miss you
like the butterfly misses the caterpillar
I miss you
like the frog misses the tadpole
I miss you
like the penguin misses the warm egg
I miss you
like my desk misses the tree it was before it was my desk
I miss you
like the oak tree misses the acorn it grew from
I miss you
like the silence misses the song
I miss you
like the book misses the blank paper
I miss you
like the surprise misses still being a surprise
I miss you
like the sailor misses the land
  like the astronaut misses the Earth
    like the grownup misses being the child
like the arrow misses the bow it's shot from
I miss you
like
I miss you

In The Dark

Lying in bed
a little afraid
listening to the noises
in the dark
in the night
in the house
the squeaks, ticks and bumps

I remember what Mum said:

think of the house as a ship
  in the night
    on the sea
    with the rigging
  creaking above
as it rocks on the waves

it's so peaceful out at sea
  no ghosts
    no monsters
    no burglars
  nothing scary
all noises explained away simply

and I lie in bed
no longer afraid
just, ever so slightly, seasick instead.

The Taste Of A Biscuit

I remembered how I used to play with my mum.
As a kid, in the kitchen, we would bake together.

Now though she's gone,
and although I'm grown up
and can care for myself, can cook for myself,
although I don't need her to wash my hair or buy my clothes
or hold my hand as I cross the road,
still it was nice to know she was always there, just in case.

Looking through her drawers after she'd died
I found, buried down, tucked away at one side
a little plastic thing, shaped like a star,
that I hadn't seen for twenty years or more,
that we used to use to cut biscuits out from rolled out dough.

And it was just this that I remembered today,
while chatting with friends about other things.
As I took a cookie to dunk in my tea
it was as if the memory just crept up on me,

and sadness came along hand in hand and hugged me.

Flowers

I think, for a moment, how loved
this lamppost must be
to be so celebrated with flowers.

Bunches of them are tied on,
taped up, and though they're wilting,
browning and dying now,

I can still see their fresh-faced floral thrill,
bright as morning, laughing
with happiness, but then

the moment passes, and I know
why people tie flowers here;
here, where, a week before,

there was broken glass and sirens,
now there is silence,
falling petals and the opposite of joy.

Alphapoem

A is for Aadvark (three 'a's in that).
B is for Bowler, a gentleman's hat.
C is for Cabbage, but not for Kitkat.

D is a Donkey you ride on the beach.
E is for Eat, what you do to a peach.
F is for Far (what's not within reach).

G is for Ghost, what you are when you're dead.
H is the thing on your shoulders, a Head.
I is for 'I'd rather go back to bed'.

J is for Jump, like a kangaroo does.
K is for Keith, who once drove a bus.
L is for Lazy at working out rhymes.

M is for Secret (I will not tell).
N's for Not knowing the alphabet well.
P is for Perfume which makes a nice smell.

S is for 'Shortly we'll come to the end'.
T is for Trevor, Simon's best friend.
V is for Vera, who has postcards to send.

X is for X-Rays, which doctors can see.
Y is for 'Why did this happen to me?'
Z is a Zebra that's stuck up a tree.

O's Over here (I had started to wonder).
Q is in hiding (it's frightened of thunder).
R joined a pirate ('Argh, matey!'), and shared in some
                                        plunder.

Two letters are missing but never mind that,
have you seen what the cat has just done in my hat?

It's made me Unhappy and made my hat Wet.
(I'm thinking that cat needs a trip to the vet.)

Troll Song

'It wasn't always my ambition to live under a bridge.
There came a point though where a decision had to
                                            be made.
It was either here or in a swamp or in a cave.

On the plus side, there's cold running water all the time.
On the minus side, I am living under a bridge.
There's little privacy and less in the way of respect.

It's only a small bridge. My feet stick out when I sleep.
I bang my head more than I'd like.
I get into arguments with ducks.

People look down on me, living under a bridge.
But it's a tradition, my mum said, and tradition's tradition.
Sometimes I eat the ducks. Those are arguments I've won.

On either river bank are pastures. Lush-lands.
I like the smell in spring of the hundred different flowers.
I never mention this when other trolls come to visit.

I read a lot of books. They contain other worlds.
For a time I can imagine I'm not living under a bridge.
You can learn things in books too, important useful things:
I eat every goat I see these days, just to be on the
                                            safe side.'

Raindrops Keep Falling Out Of Bed

As the raindrop looked out of the cloud,
at the world so green below,
so far below, such a long way down,
it said, 'I don't want to go.'

The next raindrop along,
who hadn't yet seen the view,
shoved his way to the front,
as rude raindrops are known to do.

By pushing and playing rough
the second raindrop sent
the first one out of the porthole
suddenly earthward bent.

Raindrops are pretty stupid,
like lemmings they share one brain,
where one went the rest all followed,
and the drops began to rain

all over the earth below,
the green fields lapped it up,
the river was heavily cratered,
a good day was had by ducks.

The first drop, who'd feared the fall,
opened his eyes again,
he was no longer a drop anymore,
no longer a droplet of rain.

He couldn't see where he ended
or where the next droplet began:
they were all river and river now,
and being now river they ran

downhill all the way to the ocean,
huger than all of the land.
They swam with the fish and the turtles,
with whales and with dolphins and

then the bright sun shone,
it shone for long empty hours,
and the ocean surface vanished,
lifted up in an anti-shower.

And our droplet evaporated,
passed out into dreamless sleep,
only to wake up in cold air,
in the heart of the cloud-castle keep.

The raindrop looked out of the cloud,
at the earth that rolled by below,
far below, such a long way down,
and said, 'Let's have another go.'

Pirates

The vegetarian pirate
has a carrot instead of a parrot,
which doesn't make much sense
but is handy if he ever needs
a nutritious snack halfway through the day.

Yo Ho Ho and a Bottle of Diet Coke Please If You Don't Mind, Thank You Ever So Much (a poem for polite pirates)

Fifteen men on the dead man's chest,
  the dead man's growing flatter.
You'd only fit seven on
  if some of them were fatter.

Some Mistakes

The seagull was sea sick.
The mountain goat tripped up.
The giraffe looked down.

The wasp sat on its sting.
The snake bit its lip.
The sloth let go.

I wrote this poem.
You read this poem.

Not The Best Poem In The World

If my imaginative powers were stronger
this poem would probably be longer.

Some Simple Solutions
For The Nervous

If you find high heights
make you giddy and queasy,
don't go upstairs.
That's pretty easy!

If the sight of spiders
makes you quake with fright,
don't
turn on the light.

If you're worried
the lion is going to eat you,
don't go to a place
where a lion might meet you.

If you're worried Mr Boxer is going to shout at you
because you've not done your homework,
do
your homework.

Not Exactly A Love Letter

You're the jam in my rice pudding.
(I prefer my pudding plain.)

You fill up all my thoughts.
(I've a headache in my brain.)

You're the tastiest steak there is.
(I've turned vegetarian.)

You're a happy song sung loudly.
(I'm an irritable librarian.)

You're the belt around my trousers.
(I'm sat nude in the bath.)

You're the world's best comedian.
(It only hurts when I laugh.)

You are my Pharaoh.
(I live in Ancient Greece.)

You've stolen my heart.
(I'm phoning the police.)

A Story Poem

Once upon a time there was something very interesting
and this very interesting thing was so fascinatingly interesting
that everyone rushed round to see it and to look at it
and to watch it and to point and stare and gossip about it.

And they formed a big crowd, full of colour and bustle,
swaying this way and that, murmuring with life,
swelling with curiosity, and I was much too polite
to push my way to the front and find out what was going on.

Horrible Poem

This poem is really unpleasant.
It's quite sad, too.

It's about a very, very cute kitten,
and a very, very, very cute puppy
who are best of bestest friends.

And then they get eaten by a monster.

You know, the sort that hangs around
underneath beds or behind wardrobes
waiting for cute animals to just wander by.

The poem doesn't have much story in it.

In fact, it's mainly just a load of noises.
Horrible scrunching, crunching noises...

(SKru-NCH...

Krun-CH-ch-CH!)

and squelching, krelching, belching noises...

(SSPLL-Untch...

SQUI-lch-TCH...

Gru-uRRR-PP!).

Dreadful stuff, with wet dribbling drobblets
and retching, coughing and smushing sounds,
as bones crunch and fur gets spat out
and a tail wags frantically before vanishing
down the dark hole of the monster's great gullet.

In the middle of all that
is a tiny meow

(me-ow...)

and then it's straight back to the

smashing, cracking, crackling and slurping,
the carrumphing, gulping, yelping and burping...

(brrRR-uuUrgPP-P-P-P!)

the slick slippery slunching of a slimy tongue
and the popping, slopping, sploinch

(SPLOINCH!)

of a happy monster swallowing the last mouthful
of his favourite meal of the day:

a mixed kitten and puppy takeaway.

Like I said, it's not a nice poem,
in fact, if you're squeamish,
I'd turn away at the top of the page
before the poem even begins.

Some Wigyiig Facts

The wigyiig is a monster
of which I'm sure you've heard.

It's scaly like a badger,
breathes fire like a bird.

It's green as any carrot,
slightly older than a chair.

It's wiser than a duck or swan
and lives just over there.

Never look it in the ear,
and never wash your feet

(a wigyiig sniffs deeply
when deciding who to eat).

If I Woke Up As A Beetle

If I woke up as a beetle
my bed would be too big.
My breakfast wouldn't interest me,
I couldn't give a fig —

a cornflake twice the size of me?
I'd be scared I'd drop it
and if mum saw a beetle on the table,
well, she'd attempt to swat it.

I wouldn't have to go to school though
'cause when I raised my hand
my teacher wouldn't notice me
and besides she wouldn't understand

because beetles can't speak English
and the English can't speak Beetle.
So I'll stay at home instead
and if the weather's nice my feet'll

walk me round the garden
where I'll chat with other bugs
and worms and centipedes
and with snails and flies and slugs.

My Mad Uncle, My Aunts and The Endless Scarf

My aunts aren't really too bad.
They're a level-headed bunch.
But my uncle is totally mad.
He eats baguettes for lunch.

But that isn't why he's odd.
Lots of folks do that.
It's how he likes to plod
in the quad without a hat.

The rules clearly state:
all heads must please be covered.
No wonder my aunts (all eight)
wish they'd never been brothered.

But solemnly they sit
and watch the chap parade.
They sit and start to knit
and talk of things they've made:

the Endless Woolly Scarf
and a cosy for his beard.
They've drawn a little graph
which is clearly to be feared.

It shows how day by day
the Endless Scarf keeps growing.
They knit it, come what may
(even when it isn't snowing).

Now it trips you in the street
and it trips you on the stairs.
It tangles round the feet.
It will catch you unawares.

That woolly snake's a danger.
It has clogged the motorway.
The Prime Minister (never a stranger
to having a thing to say)

has made a speech about it,
introduced an anti-scarf law.
My aunts continue to flout it.
I think this is leading to war.

They knit as the tanks start to rumble.
The scarf clogs up in their tracks.
The soldiers trip and stumble.
They're lying in wool on their backs.

The needles are clicking and clacking.
The scarf is spooling away.
The army is taking a whacking.
It's wrapped up by the end of the day.

So, we live in a warm cosy world now.
We climb through the tangles of scarf.
And to think I said at the start
that my uncle was mad! How daft!

Postcards From The Hedgehog

i.
Dear Mum,

Beautiful weather.
I saw a fox last night,
did as you always said
and rolled into a ball.
After a while it went away.
I was a bit scared all the same.
Wish you were here,

love Simon.

ii.
Dear Mum,

Lovely weather today.
Just saw a really pretty girl.
Not sure how to approach her.
She makes me really shy
but just all warm inside.
I rolled up into a ball.
Wish you were here,

love Simon.

iii.
Dear Mum,

It's raining today. I ate a slug.
Wasn't as good as the ones
you used to give us.
Tomorrow I think I'll approach the girl.
Perhaps I'll take her a slug.
She makes me ever so nervous.
I rolled up into a ball.
Wish you were here,

love Simon.

iv.
Dear Mum,

Sun's come out again.
This morning I was very brave
and I went to see her.
I edged up very carefully as you suggested,
but when I spoke to her
I discovered she was actually a pine-cone.
I felt very embarrassed.
Rolled up into a ball.
Wish you were here,

love Simon.

Psychic

Norman was a normal boy,
except he could see inside the heads
of the other kids —
he was psychic like that,
a telepathic terror.

He could have sworn to use his power for good,
like any decent superhero would,
but no —
he learnt all the secrets
of his friends and their friends,
he knew who liked who
and who didn't like who,
and he knew where they'd hidden their dinner money,
and who thought his jokes were funny
and who just laughed politely,
and he used this information
to cause trouble daily.

He'd tell Nancy what Sarah
thought about Simon
and then he'd tell Sarah what Nancy
thought about Simon
and let them fight it out between them.

He'd play Veronica
at Top Trumps
and always win.

The dinner ladies were amazed
when day after day
he avoided the bowl of crumble and custard
they'd hidden the bogey in —
and see how he'd always hand it to little Jim
(because Norman didn't think much of him).

But when exam day came round
Norman found his comeuppance come round too.
He didn't revise
or look through his books
or listen in class
because he'd a plan —
he'd look into the mind
of the boy sat next to him,
steal his answers
and pass like that, but
he found he was sat next to Bernie
who was astonishingly,
naturally
and brilliantly
dim.

It was nice to see Norman cry
when the results came in.

A Poem About Some Food

I eat pizza. I eat bread.
I eat toast when I'm in bed.

I eat soup with a ladle.
I eat meat at the table.

I eat apples. I eat pears.
I eat fruit in many chairs.

I eat beans. I eat rice.
I eat anything that's nice.

I eat cows. I eat sheep.
I eat chickens going cheep.

I eat pasta. I eat peas.
I things that live in trees.

I eat squirrels. I eat birds.
I have seconds. I have thirds.

I eat lettuce. I eat carrots.
I eat multi-coloured parrots.

I eat anything that moves.
I eat trotters. I eat hooves.

I eat legs and I eat thighs.
I eat brains and I eat eyes.

I eat hearts and I eat lungs.
Given gravy I'd eat tongues.

I eat spiders. I eat flies.
I eat worms when baked in pies.

I eat crisps and I eat biscuits.
Eat a hedgehog? Of course I'd risk it.

I eat things that I can't name.
When I get sick I don't know what to blame.
So I eat it all again.

I eat hot things. I eat cold.
But I won't do as I am told.

'Eat your sprouts,' my mother said.
Brussells sprouts? I'd rather be dead.

Midnight Feasting

I'm slipping on my slippers
and I'm slipping out of bed.
I creep into the kitchen
'cause I'm wanting to be fed.

It's the middle of the night
and there's no one else around
so I can eat what I like
and I eat what I've found.

There's half a pound of butter
and there's half a loaf of bread.
There're several dozen kiwi fruit —
I shove them in my head

through the hole in the front
that I like to call my mouth
and I swallow them directly
and they're all heading south.

There're kippers in the fridge
and there's treacle on the side —
I dip the one into the other
and I send them for a ride.

There's an aubergine I munch
and a tin of rice pudding —
I open it and swallow it
and boy it is a good 'un.

But now I'm getting thirsty
so I drink a pint of milk
all mixed with mustard powder:
it slips down smooth as silk.

I follow that with cornflakes.
I follow them with mince.
I follow that with curry
and I give it all a rinse

with the cartons of juices
(both the orange and the carrot) —
in no time at all though
I'm squawking like a parrot,

'cause I'm feeling rather odd
and I'm feeling rather sick.
I creep back up the stairs
like an old man with a stick.

As I climb into my bed
I'm feeling rather fragile
like somebody's been hitting
my stomach with a cudgel.

I don't regret I did it though.
I don't regret a thing.
And while I am turning greener
at least I get to sing

'I'm slipping on my slippers
and I'm slipping out of bed...'
and the rest of the song
is the poem you've just read.

Song Of The Fussy Eater

I don't want any milk today,
I don't want any porridge,
I don't want any mushrooms,
all that stuff is horrid.

Feed it to the dustman,
or to a chimpanzee,
feed it to my mum or dad,
just don't feed it to me.

I don't want any peas today,
I don't want any cabbage,
I don't want semolina,
all that stuff is rubbish.

Feed it to the postman,
or to the new MP,
feed it to my brother,
just don't feed it to me.

I don't want any sprouts today,
I don't care if they're just in,
I don't want any vegetables,
all that stuff's disgusting.

Feed it to my teachers,
or to sailors out at sea,
feed it all to anyone,
just don't feed it to me.

I don't want any chocolate,
I...

Oh, hang on.

That's not right!

Um...

I would quite like some chocolate,
I've a soft spot for ice cream,
I rather fancy a doughnut
but I do not want to seem

fussy or unhelpful
so I'll nibble the broccoli edge.
I'm not allowed dessert
until I've eaten some of my veg.

I Want To Be A Wallaby
(Or A Kangaroo)

to be read aloud at high speed, getting faster

I wanna be a wallaby
I wanna be a wallaby
I wanna be a wallaby
or else a kangaroo.

I wanna be a wallaby
I wanna be a wallaby
I wanna be a wallaby
or else a kangaroo.

A kangaroo can do what a wallaby can
and a wallaby can do what a kangaroo does.
When kangaroos do what the wallabies do
the wallabies don't worry 'cause they do it too.

And I...
    wanna be a wallaby
I wanna be a wallaby
I wanna be a wallaby
or else a kangaroo.

I wanna be a wallaby
I wanna be a wallaby
I wanna be a wallaby
or else a kangaroo.

I'd bounce, bounce, bounce, bounce, bounce, bounce,
                                                bounce,
bounce all around, then I'd bounce some more,
I'd bounce, bounce, bounce, bounce, bounce, bounce,
                                                bounce,
I'd bounce to the park and I'd bounce to the store,
I'd bounce, bounce, bounce, bounce, bounce, bounce,
                                                bounce,
bounce, bounce, bounce, bounce, bounce, bounce, bounce,
I'd bounce,   bounce,   bounce,   bounce,
and then I'd have a sit down because I'm feeling tired.

But I...
   wanna be a wallaby
I wanna be a wallaby
I wanna be a wallaby
or else a kangaroo.

I wanna be a wallaby
I wanna be a wallaby
I wanna be a wallaby
or else a kangaroo.

A kangaroo can do what a wallaby can
and a wallaby can do what a kangaroo does.
When kangaroos do what the wallabies do
the wallabies don't worry 'cause they do it too.

I'll keep on bouncing, bouncing, bouncing,
keep on bouncing 'til I'm sick
keep on bouncing, bouncing, bouncing,
'til I've had enough of it.

repeat ad nauseum

The Visitation

I was trying to get to sleep
  when I saw the flashing lights
and I heard that high-pitched humming
  descending from the heights,

and the windows started to rattle
  as the roar got ever louder
and then there came a crash
  as dad's shed got turned to powder.

I tip-toed down the stairs
  and peered out the cat's cat-flap
at the interstellar vessel
  that had squashed the garden flat

and a figure was emerging
  from a bright white glowing hatch
and it had two arms and had two legs
  and had two heads to match.

It was wrapped up in a spacesuit
  that shimmered with unearthly powers
and it made its way toward the house
  through the wreckage of mum's flowers.

It pointed a knobbly finger,
  it must have seen me all along,
'Are you Master Jargle Flackenfrex?'
  'Not me,' I said, 'You've got it wrong.'

'Wrong?' he said. 'Oh, bother!
  Blast! I've done it again.
I'm sorry to have troubled you.'
  Then, before I could explain,

he climbed back into his spaceship,
  left the garden with a roar,
and all I wanted to tell him was
  Mr Flackenfrex lives next-door.

Outside

Find a field away from town.
Lie down.
Wait for night to put on its crown.

A jewel-box spilt on a velvet cloak.
The show no one can revoke.
Make patterns: there's a bear, a dog, a bloke.

Let the night make its mark.
Its sky's the opposite of dark.
Filled with a thousand burning sparks.

The Milky Way's a dusty sweep.
The night is deep.
It's cold. Go inside. Try to sleep.